AMANDA GORMAN

GROUNDBREAKING POET

by Rachel Rose

Consultant: Beth Gambro
Reading Specialist, Yorkville, Illinois

BEARPORT
PUBLISHING

Minneapolis, Minnesota

Teaching Tips

BEFORE READING

- Look at the cover of the book. Discuss the picture and the title.

- Ask readers to brainstorm a list of what they already know about Amanda Gorman. What can they expect to see in this book?

- Go on a picture walk, looking through the pictures to discuss vocabulary and make predictions about the text.

DURING READING

- Read for purpose. Encourage readers to look for key pieces of information they can expect to see in biographies.

- Ask readers to look for the details of the book. What happened to Amanda Gorman at different times of her life?

- If readers encounter an unknown word, ask them to look at the sounds in the word. Then, ask them to look at the rest of the page. Are there any clues to help them understand?

AFTER READING

- Encourage readers to pick a buddy and reread the book together.

- Ask readers to name three things Amanda Gorman has done throughout her life. Go back and find the pages that tell about these things.

- Ask readers to write or draw something they learned about Amanda Gorman.

Credits:
Cover and title page, ©dpa picture alliance/Alamy, 3, ©Kathy Hutchins/Shutterstock; 5, ©Rob Carr/Staff/Getty Images; 7, ©Strike First/Shutterstock; 8, ©Alto Vintage Images/Alamy; 11, ©Jamie McCarthy/Staff/Getty Images; 13, ©anek.soowannaphoom/Shutterstock; 15, ©Liderina/Shutterstock; 17, ©Shawn Miller/LOC.gov; 19, ©Rob Carr/Staff/Getty Images; 21, ©Amy Sussman/Staff/Getty Images; 22, ©Theo Wargo/Staff/Getty Images; 23, ©michaeljung/Shutterstock; 23, ©PH888/Shutterstock; 23, ©Pru Studio/Shutterstock; 23, ©Monkey Business Images/Shutterstock; 23, ©Rawpixel.com/Shutterstock; 23, ©Monkey Business Images/Shutterstock

Library of Congress Cataloging-in-Publication Data is available at www.loc.gov or upon request from the publisher.

ISBN: 978-1-63691-715-3 (hardcover)
ISBN: 978-1-63691-722-1 (paperback)
ISBN: 978-1-63691-729-0 (ebook)

For more information, write to Bearport Publishing, 5357 Penn Avenue South, Minneapolis, MN 55419. Printed in the United States of America.

Contents

Poet to a President

It was a big day for Amanda Gorman.

She stood in front of the new president.

Amanda read her **poem**.

Amanda's Life

Amanda was born in California.

She has a twin sister and a brother.

Amanda's mother raised the three of them on her own.

The city where
Amanda was born

As a child, Amanda loved to write.

She started writing songs when she was five.

Then, she started writing poems.

Amanda wrote about things that were **important** to her.

She wrote about being Black in the United States.

And she wrote about the **rights** of women.

Soon, Amanda wanted to do more.

She wanted to help children.

Amanda's work helped others learn to read.

When she was 16, Amanda started a free writing **program**.

She helped kids write about what mattered to them.

Amanda became the top **youth** poet in the United States.

She was the first person to get this **honor**.

Amanda traveled all over to read her poems.

Then, Amanda was given another big honor.

She was picked to write a poem about the United States.

Amanda read it the day Joe Biden became president.

Amanda has already done so much.

And she still wants to do a lot more.

One day, she even hopes to run for president!

Did You Know?

Born: March 7, 1998

Family: Joan Wicks (mother), Spencer (brother), Gabrielle (sister)

When she was a kid: It was hard for her to say the letter "r." She sang songs as a way to be able to say it.

Special fact: Amanda has written several books.

Amanda says: "There is always light. If only we're brave enough to see it. If only we're brave enough to be it."

Life Connections

Amanda uses her writing to show people what she cares about. What do you care about? How do you share it with others?

Glossary

honor a sign of great respect

important someone or something that matters

poem writing that often rhymes

program a plan for activities

rights the basic things that everyone should have or be able to do

youth someone who is young

Index

Read More

Briscoe, Eyrn. *Amanda Gorman (My Itty–Bitty Bio).* Ann Arbor, MI: Cherry Lake Publishing, 2022.

Hansen, Grace. *Amanda Gorman: Poet and Activist (History Maker Biographies).* Minneapolis: Abdo Kids, 2022.

Learn More Online

1. Go to **www.factsurfer.com** or scan the QR code below.
2. Enter "**Amanda Gorman**" into the search box.
3. Click on the cover of this book to see a list of websites.

About the Author

Rachel Rose is a writer who lives in California. Her favorite books to write are about people who lead inspiring lives.